Especially for
Jordan

From
Stacey

Date
2 0 1 9

Our Family
CHRISTMAS

*A Keepsake Journal of Time-Honored Traditions,
Meaningful Memories, Celebrations
of Jesus' Birth & More*

Karin Dahl Silver

BARBOUR BOOKS
An Imprint of Barbour Publishing, Inc.

Published by Barbour Books, an imprint of Barbour Publishing, Inc., P.O. Box 719, Uhrichsville, Ohio 44683, www.barbourbooks.com

Our mission is to publish and distribute inspirational products offering exceptional value and biblical encouragement to the masses.

Member of the
Evangelical Christian
Publishers Association

Printed in China.

Welcome to
Our Family Christmas,
a keepsake journal designed for all
members of the family to record
traditions and memories of Christmases
together. Family is more than how you're
related—it's found in sharing life together
and caring for each other through all the
joys and struggles life brings—and Christmas
is one of the most special times you can
share with family. As you begin this journal,
enjoy the time for togetherness as you
and your family pick out the traditions,
pictures, recipes, memories, and
family stories that will be preserved,
passed down, and cherished
for future generations.

Our Family's Christmas Traditions

After the wedding, a newlywed couple has to decide what they'll take to their new home, whether it's tangible things, like furniture and dishes, or the intangible—beliefs about God, how to live life well, and how to care for each other. Traditions distill the beliefs of families and communities into meaningful actions that are then passed on to newer members through everyone participating in them together. Christmas traditions are especially memorable in how they celebrate joyful love—the love of family and friends, and God's love in sending Jesus. How do your Christmas traditions point others to what you hold dear?

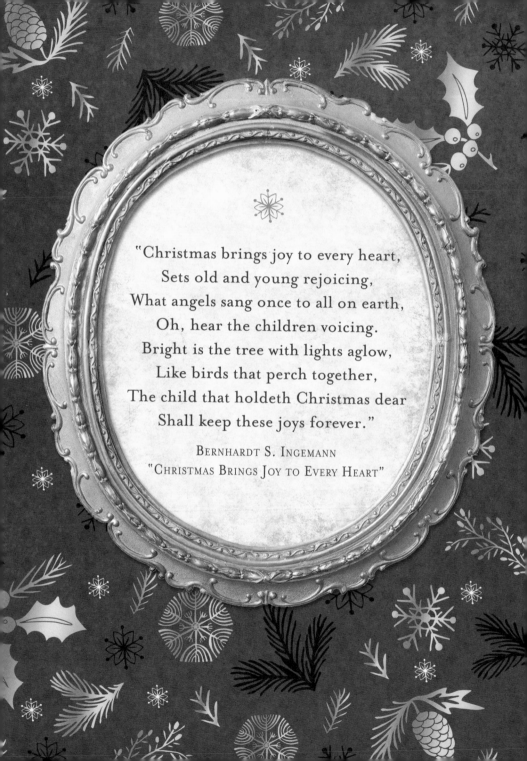

"Christmas brings joy to every heart,
Sets old and young rejoicing,
What angels sang once to all on earth,
Oh, hear the children voicing.
Bright is the tree with lights aglow,
Like birds that perch together,
The child that holdeth Christmas dear
Shall keep these joys forever."

BERNHARDT S. INGEMANN
"CHRISTMAS BRINGS JOY TO EVERY HEART"

Our Favorite Christmas Traditions from Our Childhoods

As newlyweds, how did you decide which of your individual family traditions to continue practicing together?

Christmas traditions are
meaningful to me because. . .

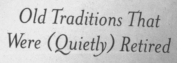

Old Traditions That Were (Quietly) Retired

New Traditions Our Family Began Celebrating and Why

....

....

....

....

....

....

....

....

....

....

....

....

....

....

....

....

But the steadfast love of the LORD is from everlasting to everlasting on those who fear him, and his righteousness to children's children, to those who keep his covenant and remember to do his commandments.

PSALM 103:17–18 ESV

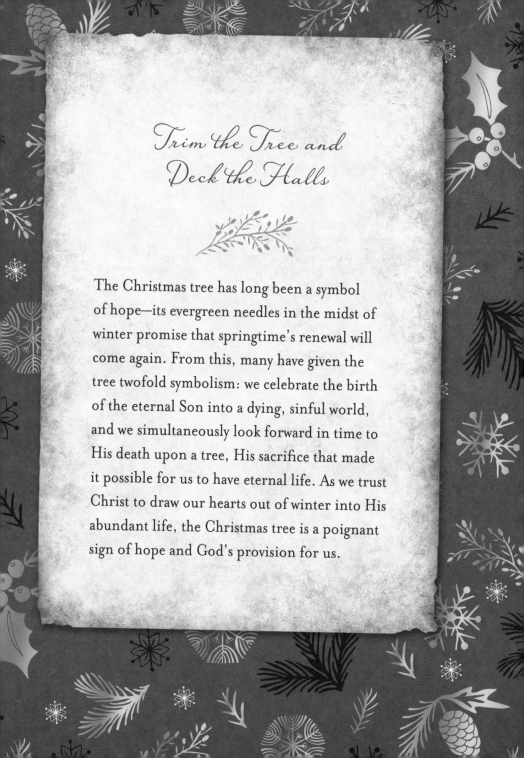

Trim the Tree and Deck the Halls

The Christmas tree has long been a symbol of hope—its evergreen needles in the midst of winter promise that springtime's renewal will come again. From this, many have given the tree twofold symbolism: we celebrate the birth of the eternal Son into a dying, sinful world, and we simultaneously look forward in time to His death upon a tree, His sacrifice that made it possible for us to have eternal life. As we trust Christ to draw our hearts out of winter into His abundant life, the Christmas tree is a poignant sign of hope and God's provision for us.

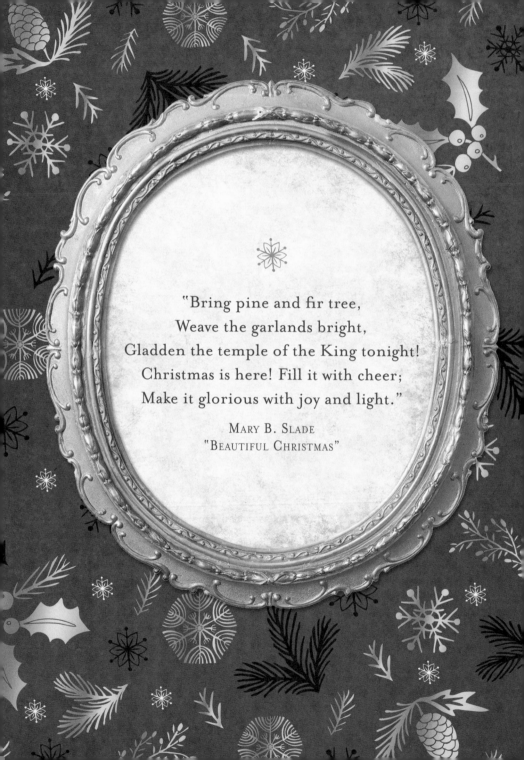

"Bring pine and fir tree,
Weave the garlands bright,
Gladden the temple of the King tonight!
Christmas is here! Fill it with cheer;
Make it glorious with joy and light."

MARY B. SLADE
"BEAUTIFUL CHRISTMAS"

Getting the Family
Christmas Tree Traditions

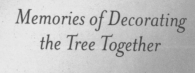

Memories of Decorating the Tree Together

Unusual Trees or Decorations Through the Years

....

....

....

....

....

....

....

....

....

....

....

....

....

....

....

....

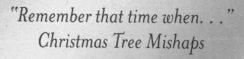

"Remember that time when. . ."
Christmas Tree Mishaps

Deck the Halls:
Christmas Decor around the House

"O Christmas tree, O Christmas tree, How sturdy God hath made thee! Thou bidds't us all place faithfully Our trust in God, unchangingly! O Christmas tree, O Christmas tree, How sturdy God hath made thee!"

ERNST ANSCHÜTZ
"O CHRISTMAS TREE"

Baubles and Lights: Christmas Ornaments and Their Stories

Sparkling glass balls and twinkling lights, tinsel and gingerbread men. . . At Christmas, we decorate our homes and hang ornaments on the tree to fill our hearts with beauty, joy, and memories of loved ones. The kids and pets are often so (dangerously) transfixed by the beautiful tree that sometimes they attempt to climb it to get a better look! Though we chide them and clean up the mess, there is something to be learned from their wonder. If only we would experience that same wonder and desire to get closer whenever we behold the beauty of Christ!

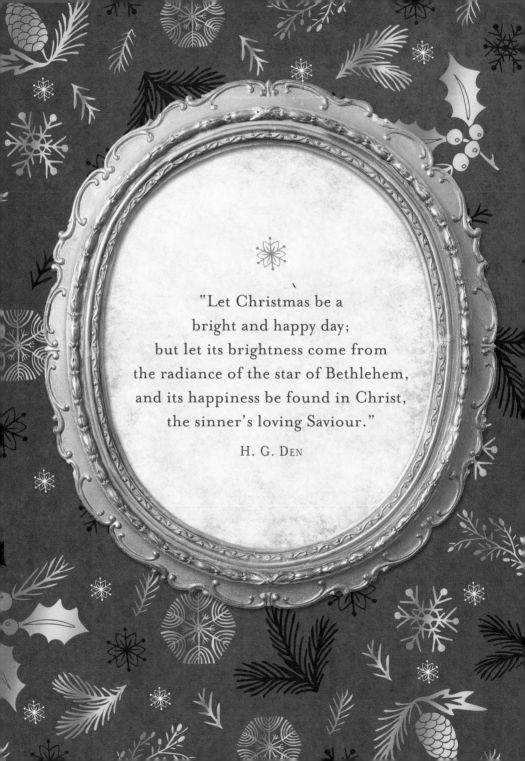

"Let Christmas be a
bright and happy day;
but let its brightness come from
the radiance of the star of Bethlehem,
and its happiness be found in Christ,
the sinner's loving Saviour."

H. G. DEN

Your Favorite Ornaments and Why

The Stories behind
Handmade Ornaments

....

....

....

....

....

....

....

....

....

....

....

....

....

....

An Untimely End:
Decoration Mishaps

Ideas for Crafts and Homemade Decorations

It feels like Christmas in the house when. . .

....

....

....

....

....

....

....

....

....

....

....

....

....

....

....

....

"So now is come our joyfull'st feast;
Let every man be jolly;
Each room with ivy leaves is drest,
And every post with holly."

GEORGE WITHER
"A CHRISTMAS CAROL"

Advent: The Season of Expectant Preparation

Just as Anna the prophetess and Simeon rejoiced to see the infant Savior after so many years of patient expectation (Luke 2:22–40), we celebrate with them as we look back on the First Advent. In many nations, the Advent season is a time of preparation, fasting, and repentance. As we prepare our homes for Christmas, we should prepare our hearts for the joyous celebration of the arrival of Emmanuel, "God with Us." As you record your family's Advent traditions, think of the many faithful believers who prayed unfailingly for the Messiah to come. . .and consider how we are to pray in faith and expectation for His Second Advent.

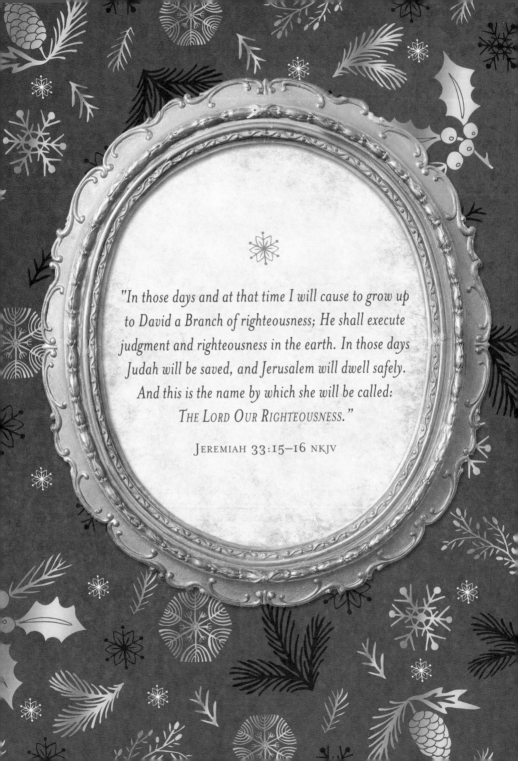

"In those days and at that time I will cause to grow up to David a Branch of righteousness; He shall execute judgment and righteousness in the earth. In those days Judah will be saved, and Jerusalem will dwell safely. And this is the name by which she will be called: THE LORD OUR RIGHTEOUSNESS."

JEREMIAH 33:15–16 NKJV

Preparing for Christmas in the Heart

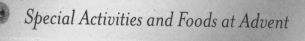

Special Activities and Foods at Advent

....

....

....

....

....

....

....

....

....

....

....

....

....

....

....

....

Marking the Time:
Advent Calendars and Wreaths

Send Out the Post!
Christmas Cards and Letters

Favorite Scripture Passages to Read for Advent

And there shall come forth a rod out of the stem of Jesse, and a Branch shall grow out of his roots: And the spirit of the LORD shall rest upon him, the spirit of wisdom and understanding, the spirit of counsel and might, the spirit of knowledge and of the fear of the LORD.

ISAIAH 11:1–2 KJV

Our Favorite Things
about Christmas

What are the things about Christmas you miss most as the New Year begins? Perhaps it's the gentle light from the Christmas tree, the warmth of cocoa to fight the cold snap in the air, familiar carols on the radio and Christmas movies, giggles under the mistletoe. Remember that God rejoices over His children (Zephaniah 3:17), and He, our loving Father, rejoices to see us enjoy Him and His creation. May you cultivate a grateful heart during the Christmas season for the things that fill you with joy. Take time to thank the Father for each one of your Christmas favorites!

The heavens are Yours,
the earth also is Yours;
the world and all its fullness,
You have founded them.

PSALM 89:11 NKJV

Our Family's Favorite Christmas Songs and Hymns

It's a Wonderful Film: Christmas Movies

Read It Again!
Christmas Books and Poems

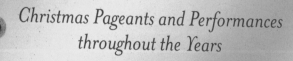

Christmas Pageants and Performances throughout the Years

Games and Crafts
for Christmastime

Winter Wonderland: Outdoor Activities and Festivals

Frolic and Festivity: Christmas Parties

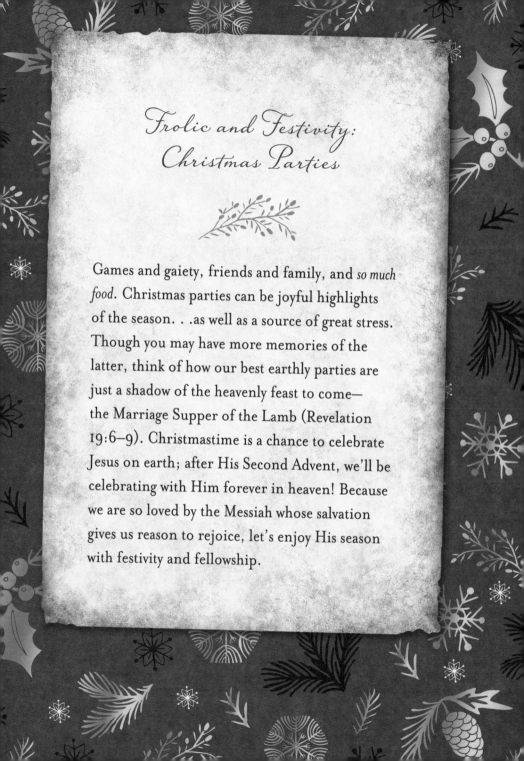

Games and gaiety, friends and family, and *so much food*. Christmas parties can be joyful highlights of the season. . .as well as a source of great stress. Though you may have more memories of the latter, think of how our best earthly parties are just a shadow of the heavenly feast to come—the Marriage Supper of the Lamb (Revelation 19:6–9). Christmastime is a chance to celebrate Jesus on earth; after His Second Advent, we'll be celebrating with Him forever in heaven! Because we are so loved by the Messiah whose salvation gives us reason to rejoice, let's enjoy His season with festivity and fellowship.

"At Christmas play and make good cheer,
For Christmas comes but once a year."

THOMAS TUSSER

How We Throw a Christmas Party

....

....

....

....

....

....

....

....

....

....

....

....

....

....

....

....

....

....

....

....

....

My favorite part of
Christmas parties is. . .

Games Galore for Kids and Adults

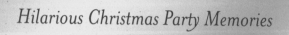

Hilarious Christmas Party Memories

Recipes for Our Best Party Goodies

"Be merry all, be merry all,
With holly dress the festive hall;
Prepare the song, the feast, the ball,
To welcome merry Christmas."

W. R. Spencer

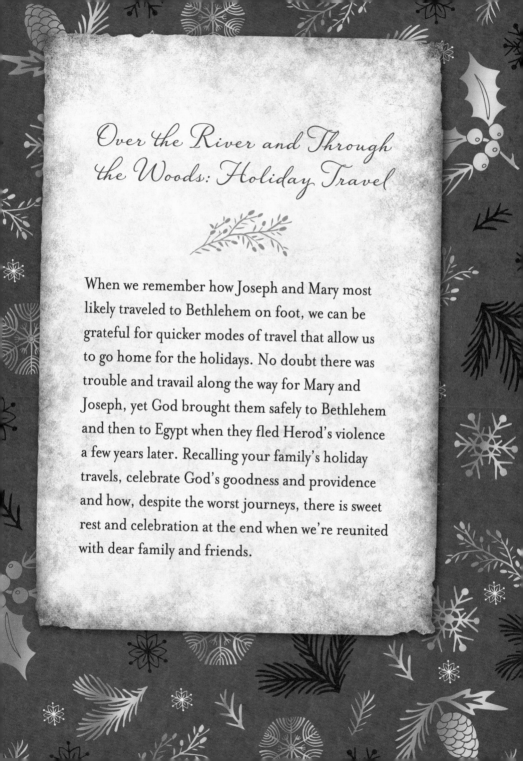

Over the River and Through the Woods: Holiday Travel

When we remember how Joseph and Mary most likely traveled to Bethlehem on foot, we can be grateful for quicker modes of travel that allow us to go home for the holidays. No doubt there was trouble and travail along the way for Mary and Joseph, yet God brought them safely to Bethlehem and then to Egypt when they fled Herod's violence a few years later. Recalling your family's holiday travels, celebrate God's goodness and providence and how, despite the worst journeys, there is sweet rest and celebration at the end when we're reunited with dear family and friends.

"We often travel on a hard and uneven road; but with a cheerful spirit, and a heart to praise God for His mercies, we may walk therein with comfort, and come to the end of our journey in peace."

DEWEY

Memories of Christmas Travels

Holiday Travel Horror Stories

....

....

....

....

....

....

....

....

....

....

....

....

....

....

....

....

....

....

Christmas with Mom's Family

Christmas with Dad's Family

The Best Parts of Christmases Away from Home

....

....

....

....

....

....

....

....

....

....

....

....

....

....

....

....

....

....

....

The LORD keeps you from all harm and watches over your life. The LORD keeps watch over you as you come and go, both now and forever.

PSALM 121:7–8 NLT

Christmas Eve: O Holy Night

We don't know much about the first Christmas Eve. After traveling to Bethlehem for the census, Mary and Joseph were likely footsore and tired. With Mary's delivery so near, they were also probably frustrated that there was no place for them to stay other than a stable. Yet they continued faithfully, trusting God, not knowing that soon the angels would light up the sky with joyful singing for the Messiah's birth. Whatever cares we carry during the Christmas season, we too ought to continue in prayerful faith as we look forward to a special day of celebrating the birth of our Lord together with family.

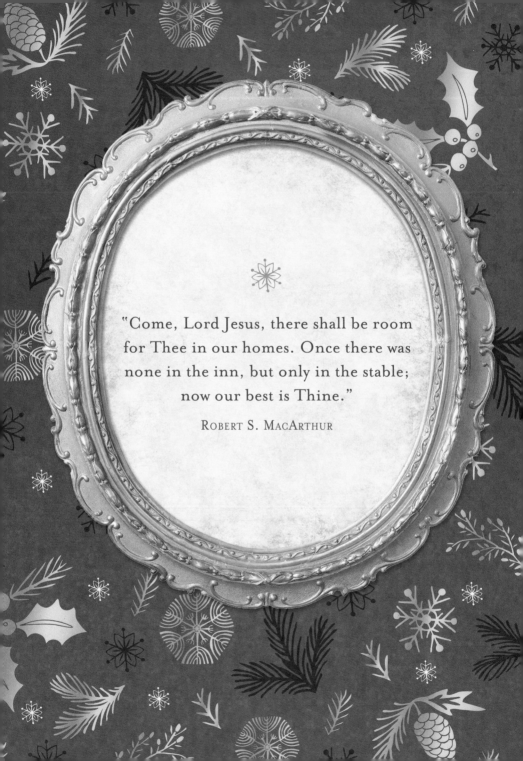

"Come, Lord Jesus, there shall be room for Thee in our homes. Once there was none in the inn, but only in the stable; now our best is Thine."

ROBERT S. MacARTHUR

Our Christmas Eve Traditions

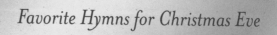

Favorite Hymns for Christmas Eve

My favorite part of Christmas Eve is. . .

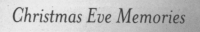

Christmas Eve Memories

Christmas Eve Wishes and Secrets

Write a prayer asking God for joyful anticipation for this Christmas Eve and those to come.

Christmas Day: The Christ Is Born!

"Don't be afraid!" he said. "I bring you good news that will bring great joy to all people. The Savior—yes, the Messiah, the Lord—has been born today in Bethlehem, the city of David!" (Luke 2:10–11 NLT). The first Christmas, the shepherds—the lowliest in Jewish society—were the favored few who heard the angelic proclamation of the Savior's birth. The Redeemer came not in a clap of thunder, but quietly—born to a humble woman in even humbler surroundings. The King of kings selflessly set aside His glory to enter a hurting world in human flesh—truly, "love came down at Christmas" (Christina Rossetti).

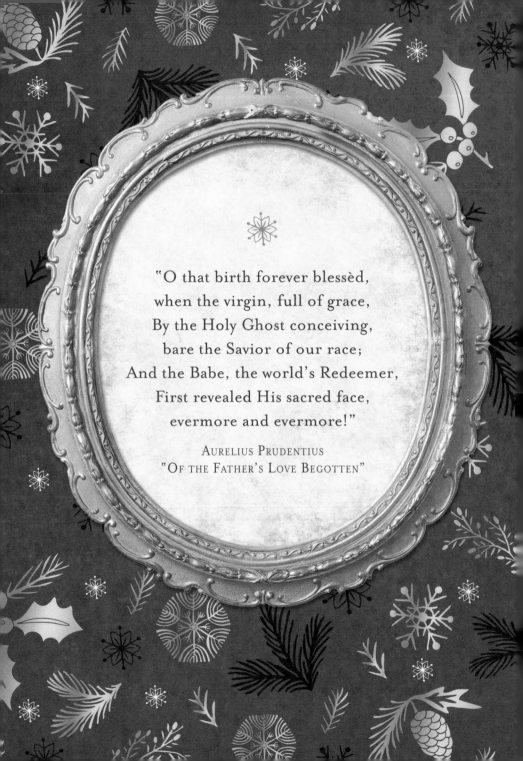

"O that birth forever blessèd,
when the virgin, full of grace,
By the Holy Ghost conceiving,
bare the Savior of our race;
And the Babe, the world's Redeemer,
First revealed His sacred face,
evermore and evermore!"

AURELIUS PRUDENTIUS
"OF THE FATHER'S LOVE BEGOTTEN"

Our Christmas Day Traditions

Unto Us a Son Is Given: Commemorating Jesus' Birth

Cherished Memories of Christmas Day

Sensational! Describe your family's Christmas Day through sight, sound, taste, smell, and touch.

How did the anticipation for Christmas change over the years in your family?

"Christians awake,
salute the happy morn
Whereon the Saviour
of the world was born."

JOHN BYROM
"HYMN FOR CHRISTMAS DAY"

Christmas Recipes and Memories from the Kitchen

Food has always been a communal joy, at Christmas most of all. It's almost scandalous to defy nature's bareness by having plenty of food in the midst of winter, but our meals are a daily opportunity to praise the One from whom all blessings flow. While we're tempted to worry over the particulars like Martha did (Luke 10:38–42), reflect on the fun in your family's traditions in preparing the Christmas feast. Record your carefully guarded recipes for Christmas foods that your family relishes, and celebrate Jesus, the Bread of Life who came down from heaven (John 6:51).

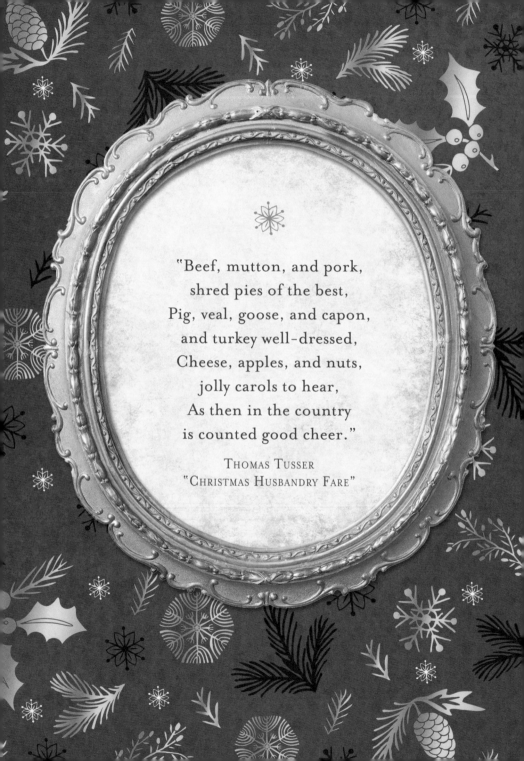

"Beef, mutton, and pork,
shred pies of the best,
Pig, veal, goose, and capon,
and turkey well-dressed,
Cheese, apples, and nuts,
jolly carols to hear,
As then in the country
is counted good cheer."

THOMAS TUSSER
"CHRISTMAS HUSBANDRY FARE"

Recipes for Christmas Goodies:
Cookies, Snacks, Drinks

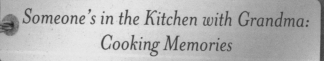

Someone's in the Kitchen with Grandma: Cooking Memories

Marvelous Main Dish Recipes

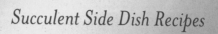

Succulent Side Dish Recipes

....

....

....

....

....

....

....

....

....

....

....

....

....

....

....

....

....

Delectable Dessert Recipes

Get Creative!
Recipes for Leftovers

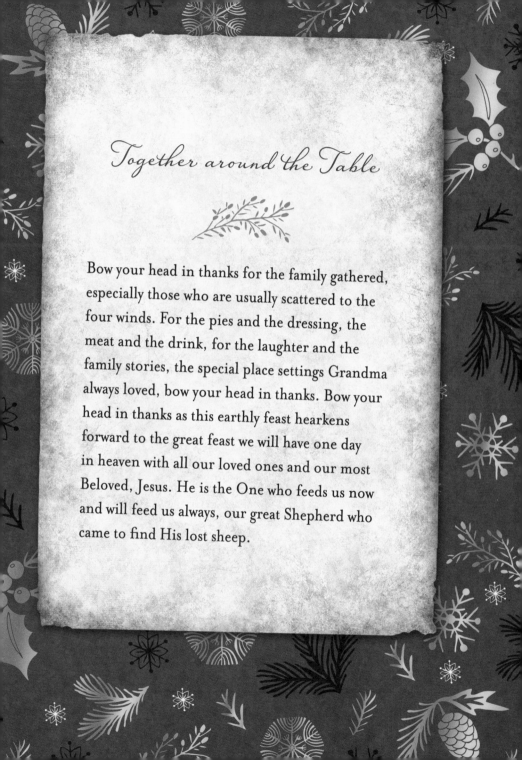

Together around the Table

Bow your head in thanks for the family gathered, especially those who are usually scattered to the four winds. For the pies and the dressing, the meat and the drink, for the laughter and the family stories, the special place settings Grandma always loved, bow your head in thanks. Bow your head in thanks as this earthly feast hearkens forward to the great feast we will have one day in heaven with all our loved ones and our most Beloved, Jesus. He is the One who feeds us now and will feed us always, our great Shepherd who came to find His lost sheep.

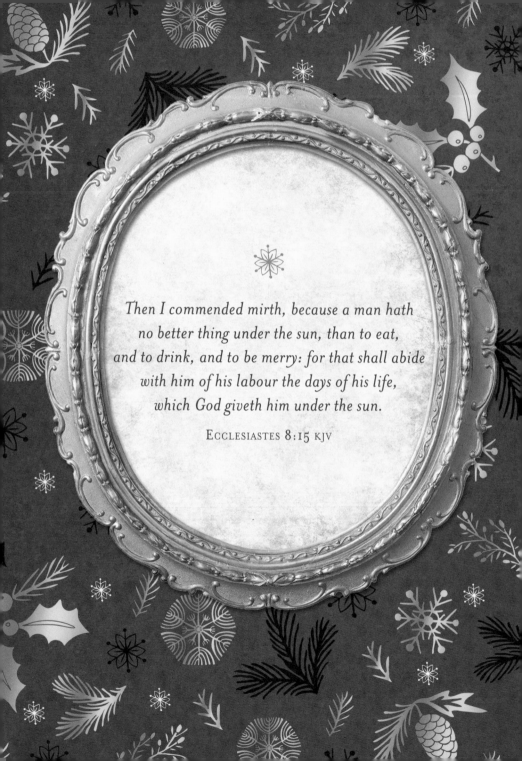

Then I commended mirth, because a man hath
no better thing under the sun, than to eat,
and to drink, and to be merry: for that shall abide
with him of his labour the days of his life,
which God giveth him under the sun.

ECCLESIASTES 8:15 KJV

Setting the Table: Memories of Preparing for Christmas Dinner

Our Favorite Foods for Christmas Eve and Christmas Day

What You Can Always Expect at Our Christmas Dinners: Traditions

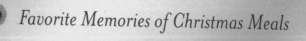

Favorite Memories of Christmas Meals

Family Stories Told around the Table

Taste and see that the LORD is good.
Oh, the joys of those who
take refuge in him!

PSALM 34:8 NLT

The Greatest Gift

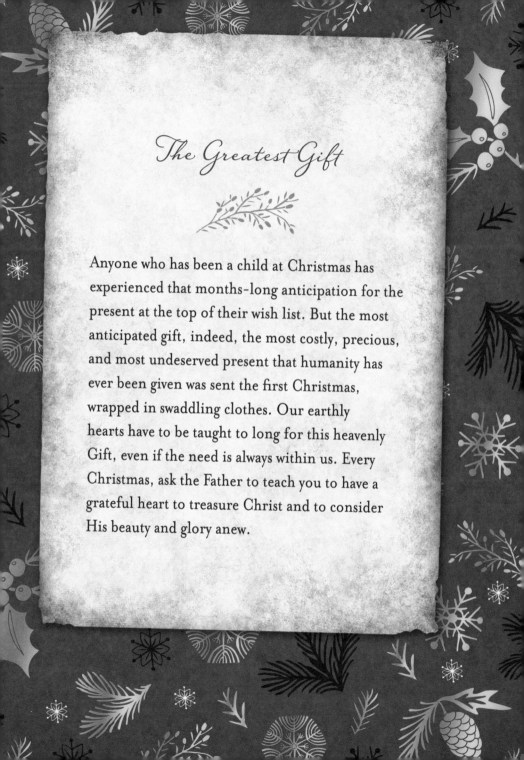

Anyone who has been a child at Christmas has experienced that months-long anticipation for the present at the top of their wish list. But the most anticipated gift, indeed, the most costly, precious, and most undeserved present that humanity has ever been given was sent the first Christmas, wrapped in swaddling clothes. Our earthly hearts have to be taught to long for this heavenly Gift, even if the need is always within us. Every Christmas, ask the Father to teach you to have a grateful heart to treasure Christ and to consider His beauty and glory anew.

For God so loved the world, that he gave his only begotten Son, that whosoever believeth in him should not perish, but have everlasting life.

JOHN 3:16 KJV

How is Jesus beautiful to you?

Jesus Gives Us the Greatest Gift

*"I give them eternal life, and they shall never perish;
no one will snatch them out of my hand."*

JOHN 10:28 NIV

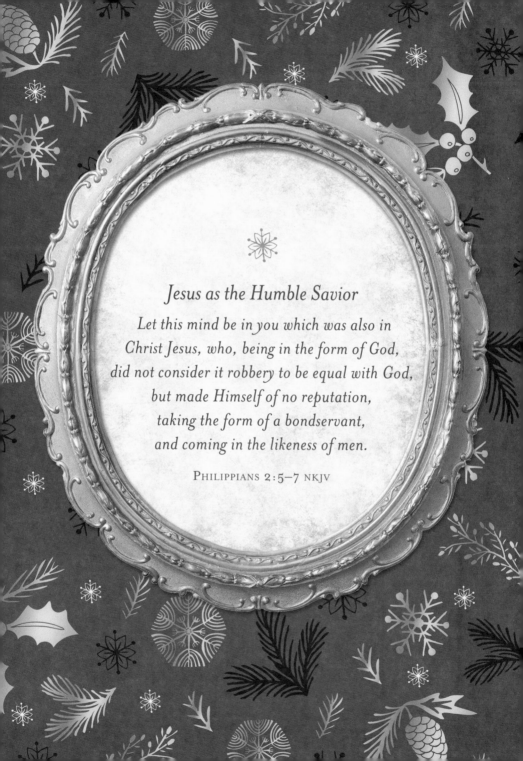

Jesus as the Humble Savior

*Let this mind be in you which was also in
Christ Jesus, who, being in the form of God,
did not consider it robbery to be equal with God,
but made Himself of no reputation,
taking the form of a bondservant,
and coming in the likeness of men.*

PHILIPPIANS 2:5–7 NKJV

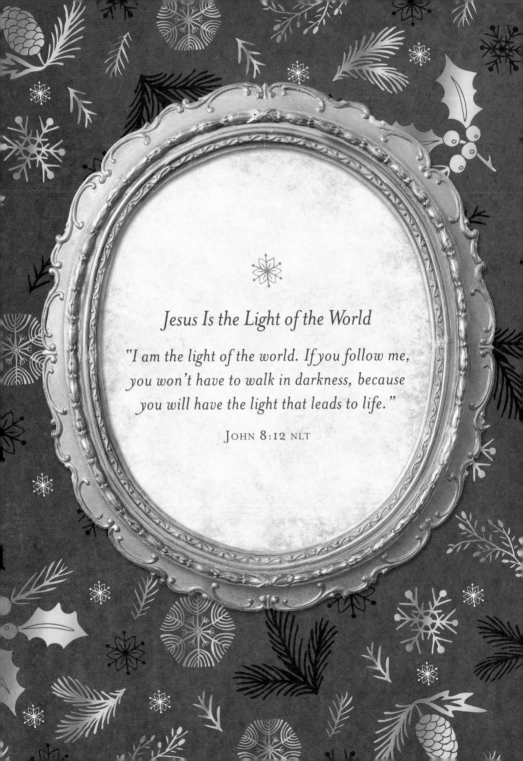

Jesus Is the Light of the World

*"I am the light of the world. If you follow me,
you won't have to walk in darkness, because
you will have the light that leads to life."*

JOHN 8:12 NLT

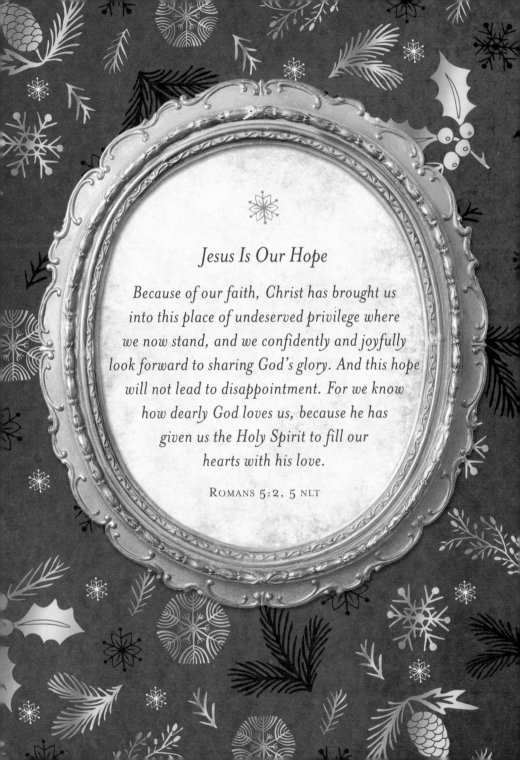

Jesus Is Our Hope

Because of our faith, Christ has brought us into this place of undeserved privilege where we now stand, and we confidently and joyfully look forward to sharing God's glory. And this hope will not lead to disappointment. For we know how dearly God loves us, because he has given us the Holy Spirit to fill our hearts with his love.

ROMANS 5:2, 5 NLT

Write a prayer asking that every
Christmas you and your family will
be renewed in thankfulness
for the gift of Jesus.

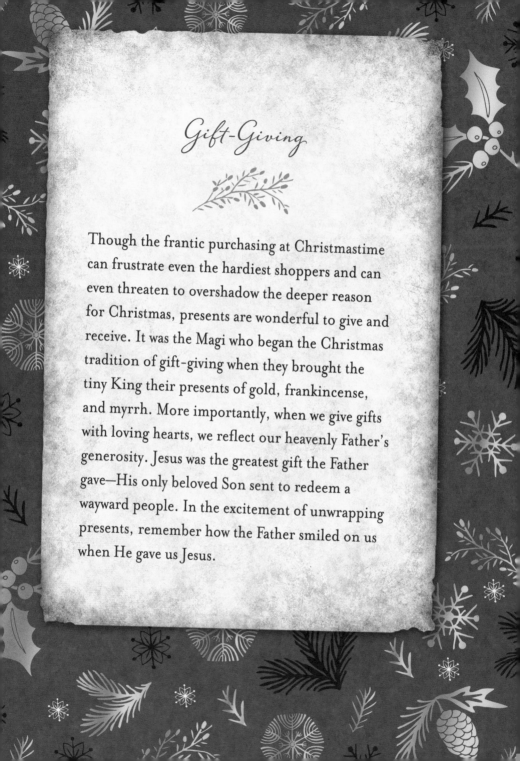

Gift-Giving

Though the frantic purchasing at Christmastime can frustrate even the hardiest shoppers and can even threaten to overshadow the deeper reason for Christmas, presents are wonderful to give and receive. It was the Magi who began the Christmas tradition of gift-giving when they brought the tiny King their presents of gold, frankincense, and myrrh. More importantly, when we give gifts with loving hearts, we reflect our heavenly Father's generosity. Jesus was the greatest gift the Father gave—His only beloved Son sent to redeem a wayward people. In the excitement of unwrapping presents, remember how the Father smiled on us when He gave us Jesus.

Every good gift and every perfect gift is from above,
and comes down from the Father of lights,
with whom there is no variation
or shadow of turning.

JAMES 1:17 NKJV

Thoughts on Family Gifts, Past and Present

Shopping, Wrapping, and Hiding Presents

Memories of Learning to Wrap Presents

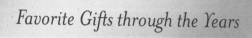

Favorite Gifts through the Years

Gifts from the Heart: Gift-giving to Others in Our Community

"When we were children we were grateful to those who filled our stockings at Christmas time. Why are we not grateful to God for filling our stockings with legs?"

G. K. CHESTERTON

Keeping Jesus at the Center of Christmas

Though many are concerned about the "war on Christmas," more important than one day of celebrating Christ's birth is celebrating His life, death, and resurrection during the whole year by loving, forgiving, and serving others. God's grand redemption story woven throughout the Bible was flung into motion by Jesus' humble entry into earthly existence—the cross was the goal, a climactic finishing blow to Satan's reign over the earth. At Christmas and always, point to the Christ who came to deliver His creation from sin, to Him who "*reconcile[d] to himself all things. . .by making peace through his blood*" (Colossians 1:20 NIV).

The Son is the image of the invisible God,
the firstborn over all creation. For in him all
things were created: things in heaven and on earth,
visible and invisible, whether thrones or powers or
rulers or authorities; all things have been created
through him and for him. He is before all things,
and in him all things hold together.

COLOSSIANS 1:15–17 NIV

Favorite Scriptures about Jesus

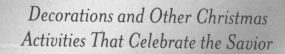

Decorations and Other Christmas
Activities That Celebrate the Savior

The Most Memorable
Christmas Pageants Ever

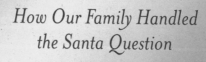

How Our Family Handled
the Santa Question

Write a prayer asking to keep Jesus at the center of your family's Christmas and thanking Him for bringing all the good things that are at Christmas—family, togetherness, peace, and reconciliation.

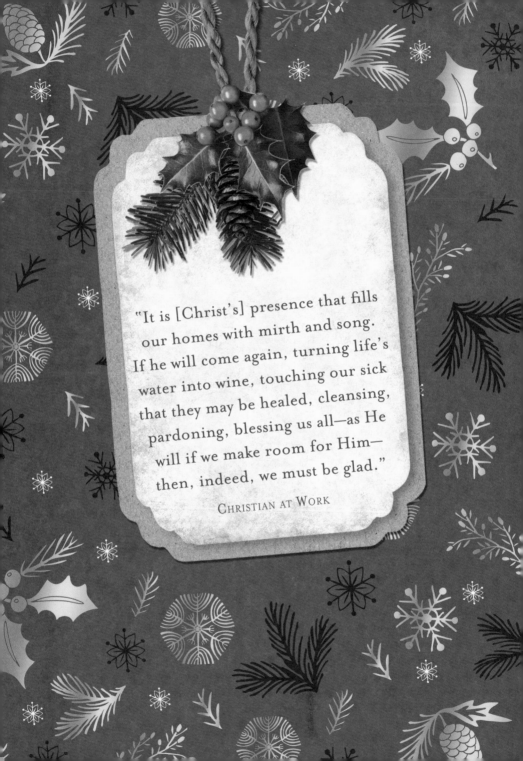

"It is [Christ's] presence that fills our homes with mirth and song. If he will come again, turning life's water into wine, touching our sick that they may be healed, cleansing, pardoning, blessing us all—as He will if we make room for Him—then, indeed, we must be glad."

CHRISTIAN AT WORK

Seeing Ourselves in the Story

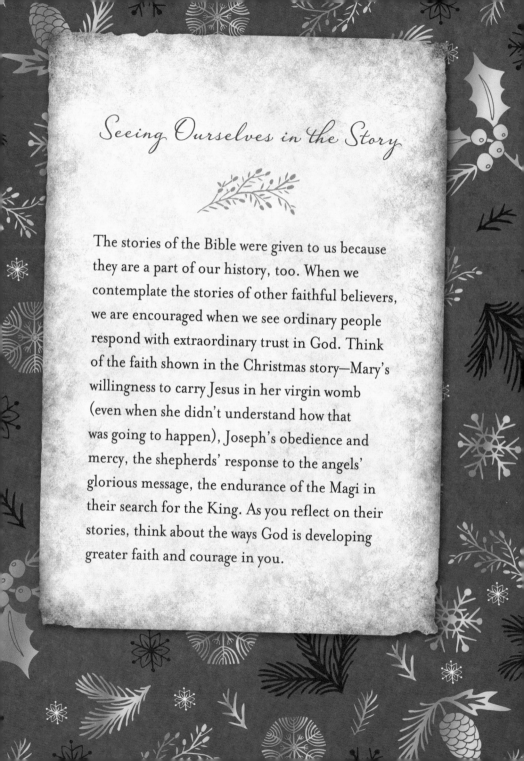

The stories of the Bible were given to us because they are a part of our history, too. When we contemplate the stories of other faithful believers, we are encouraged when we see ordinary people respond with extraordinary trust in God. Think of the faith shown in the Christmas story—Mary's willingness to carry Jesus in her virgin womb (even when she didn't understand how that was going to happen), Joseph's obedience and mercy, the shepherds' response to the angels' glorious message, the endurance of the Magi in their search for the King. As you reflect on their stories, think about the ways God is developing greater faith and courage in you.

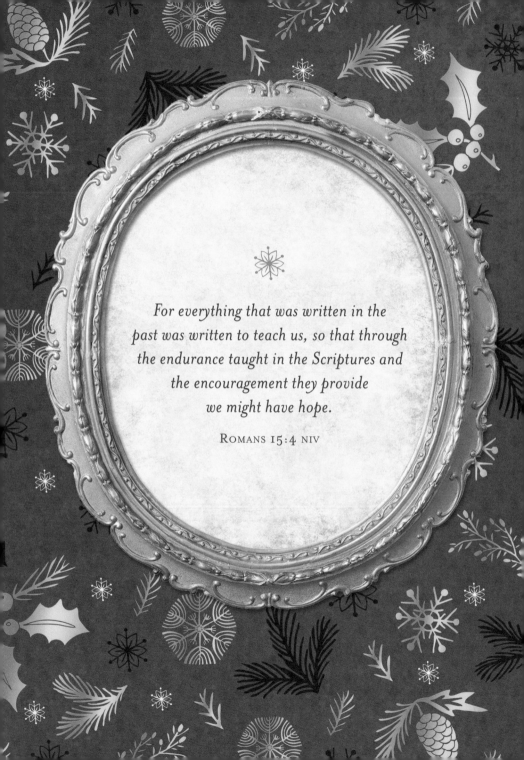

For everything that was written in the
past was written to teach us, so that through
the endurance taught in the Scriptures and
the encouragement they provide
we might have hope.

ROMANS 15:4 NIV

How would you have reacted if you were in Mary and Joseph's place?

What do you imagine it would have been like to be there with the shepherds when the angels appeared?

Write selections from your favorite praise songs or hymns that you would have sung to add to the angels' praise on the first Christmas.

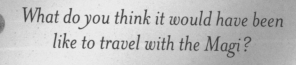

What do you think it would have been like to travel with the Magi?

....

....

....

....

....

....

....

....

....

....

....

....

....

....

....

....

....

....

How are you a part of the
Christmas story today?

"Come, then, let us hasten yonder;
Here let all, great and small,
kneel in awe and wonder,
Love Him Who with
love is yearning;
Hail the star that from far
bright with hope is burning."

CATHERINE WINKWORTH,
"ALL MY HEART THIS NIGHT REJOICES"

Serving at Christmas

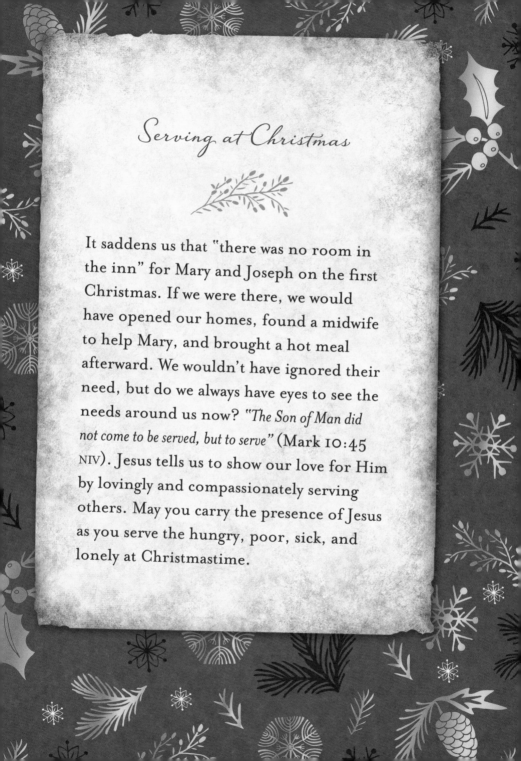

It saddens us that "there was no room in the inn" for Mary and Joseph on the first Christmas. If we were there, we would have opened our homes, found a midwife to help Mary, and brought a hot meal afterward. We wouldn't have ignored their need, but do we always have eyes to see the needs around us now? *"The Son of Man did not come to be served, but to serve"* (Mark 10:45 NIV). Jesus tells us to show our love for Him by lovingly and compassionately serving others. May you carry the presence of Jesus as you serve the hungry, poor, sick, and lonely at Christmastime.

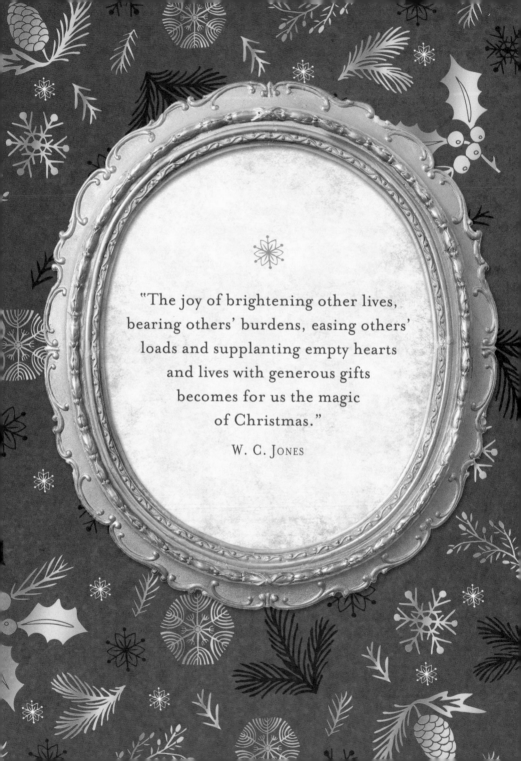

"The joy of brightening other lives, bearing others' burdens, easing others' loads and supplanting empty hearts and lives with generous gifts becomes for us the magic of Christmas."

W. C. JONES

Looking to His Example:
Christ's Miracles That Inspire Us

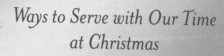

Ways to Serve with Our Time at Christmas

Write a prayer after reflecting on this quote:

"This is the meaning of Christmas; and as we love God with soul and mind and strength, and prove our divine sonship by good will and kindness toward all our fellow-men, we shall realize the divine idea of our Master and unite in His blessed work."

OBSERVER

....
....
....
....
....
....
....
....
....
....
....
....
....
....
....

"Christmas! 'Tis the season for
kindling the fire of hospitality
in the hall, the genial flame
of charity in the heart."

WASHINGTON IRVING

It Came Upon a Midnight Clear

Many have debated the actual season in which Jesus was born, though hymns and songs often set the scene in the cold of winter. More important than knowing the date is the fact that the Creator was born that night as a little baby. He who had made all things with a word would now experience the weather from an earthly perspective—He would quiet storms on the Sea of Galilee and the storms in the hearts of those who love Him. Christ's people can take heart that they are safe in His care, regardless of whether Christmas is snowy or sunny.

"Heap on more wood! the wind is chill;
But let it whistle as it will,
We'll keep our Christmas merry still."

SIR WALTER SCOTT

White Christmases: Memories (or Dreams)

How has climate or weather affected the way your family celebrates Christmas?

Outdoor Fun at Christmastime

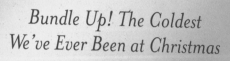

Bundle Up! The Coldest We've Ever Been at Christmas

In my opinion, the ideal weather
for Christmas is. . .

"It is coming, Old Earth,
it is coming tonight!
On the snowflakes
which cover thy sod
The feet of the Christ-child
fall gentle and white,
And the voice of the Christ-child
tells out with delight
That mankind are
the children of God."

PHILLIPS BROOKS, "CHRISTMAS CAROL"

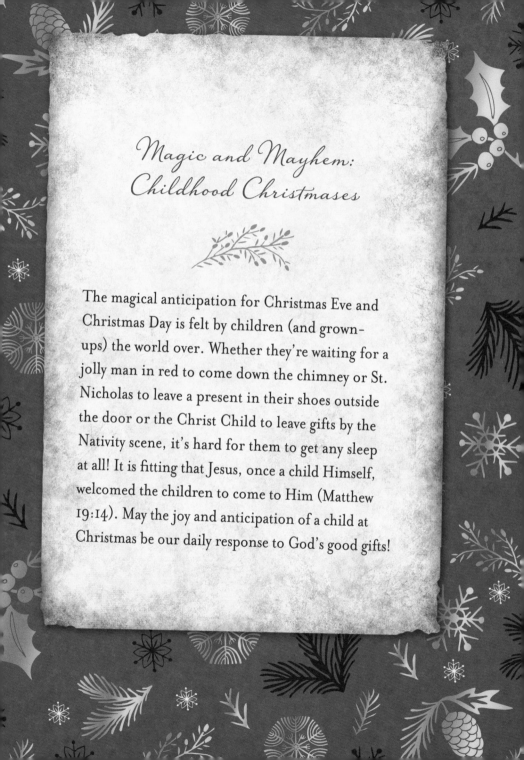

Magic and Mayhem: Childhood Christmases

The magical anticipation for Christmas Eve and Christmas Day is felt by children (and grown-ups) the world over. Whether they're waiting for a jolly man in red to come down the chimney or St. Nicholas to leave a present in their shoes outside the door or the Christ Child to leave gifts by the Nativity scene, it's hard for them to get any sleep at all! It is fitting that Jesus, once a child Himself, welcomed the children to come to Him (Matthew 19:14). May the joy and anticipation of a child at Christmas be our daily response to God's good gifts!

"It is good to be children sometimes,
and never better than at Christmas,
when its mighty Founder was
a child Himself."

CHARLES DICKENS

Favorite Christmas Memories
from Childhood

....

....

....

....

....

....

....

....

....

....

....

....

....

....

....

....

....

....

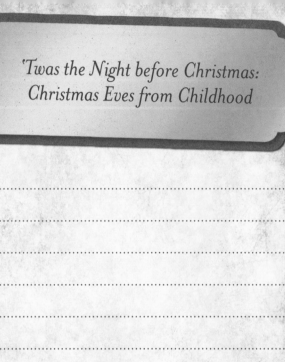

'Twas the Night before Christmas:
Christmas Eves from Childhood

I knew I was growing up when _____ started changing about Christmas. . .

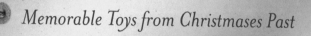

Memorable Toys from Christmases Past

What I Thought about Santa as a Kid

"For little children everywhere
A joyous season still we make;
We bring our precious gifts
to them, even for the dear
child Jesus' sake."

PHOEBE GARY
"CHRISTMAS"

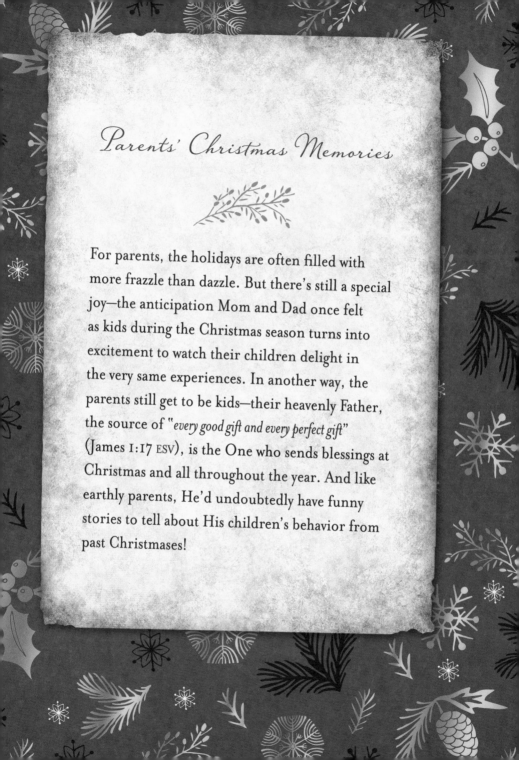

Parents' Christmas Memories

For parents, the holidays are often filled with more frazzle than dazzle. But there's still a special joy—the anticipation Mom and Dad once felt as kids during the Christmas season turns into excitement to watch their children delight in the very same experiences. In another way, the parents still get to be kids—their heavenly Father, the source of *"every good gift and every perfect gift"* (James 1:17 ESV), is the One who sends blessings at Christmas and all throughout the year. And like earthly parents, He'd undoubtedly have funny stories to tell about His children's behavior from past Christmases!

Let your father and mother be glad;
let her who bore you rejoice.

PROVERBS 23:25 ESV

Christmas before We Had Kids

Memories of Our Little Ones' First Christmases

Passing the Torch:
Teaching Traditions to the Kids

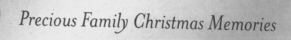

Precious Family Christmas Memories

....

....

....

....

....

....

....

....

....

....

....

....

....

....

....

....

"Remember When. . ."
Stories the Kids Won't Live Down

How Our Traditions Have Changed over the Years

Capturing the Christmas Spirit

Time seems to speed up the older you get. Children agonize as they wait for each day to pass until the weekend. . .while parents look at the calendar in astonishment to see that Christmas is in less than a month! How encouraging it is to know that God is not subject to time—He sees it all as a single snapshot of His beautiful plan. Though we are but a speck in that picture, God holds us dear, for He formed us with intention and love (Psalm 139:13–16). As time passes, it's worth looking back on special Christmas moments. Gather favorite pictures for this section, and enjoy the memories!

So teach us to number our days,
that we may apply our hearts unto wisdom.

PSALM 90:12 KJV

Family Christmas Portraits

Insert Photo Here

More Family Christmas Portraits

Insert Photo Here

If I had to pick a picture that sums
up our family at Christmas,
I'd choose. . . (and here's why).

....

....

....

....

....

....

....

....

....

....

....

....

....

....

....

....

Lots of Laughs

Insert Photo Here

It's Christmas! Say Cheese!

Insert Photo Here

Pick an old family portrait

Insert Photo Here

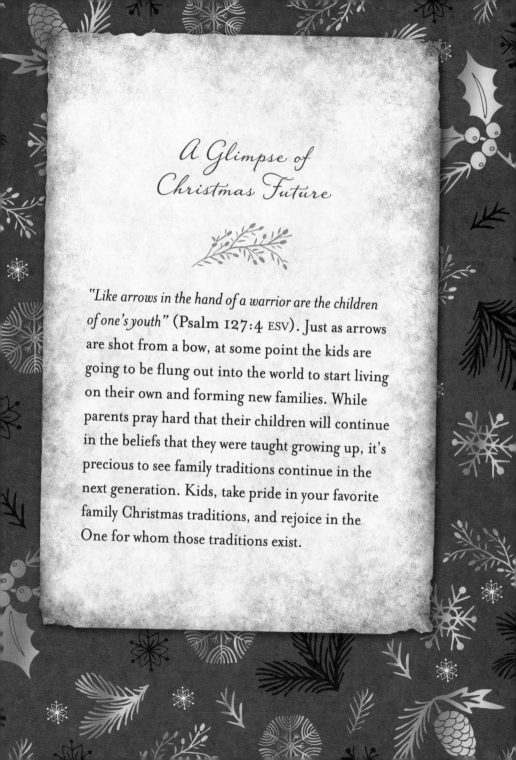

A Glimpse of Christmas Future

"Like arrows in the hand of a warrior are the children of one's youth" (Psalm 127:4 ESV). Just as arrows are shot from a bow, at some point the kids are going to be flung out into the world to start living on their own and forming new families. While parents pray hard that their children will continue in the beliefs that they were taught growing up, it's precious to see family traditions continue in the next generation. Kids, take pride in your favorite family Christmas traditions, and rejoice in the One for whom those traditions exist.

We can make our plans,
but the LORD determines our steps.

PROVERBS 16:9 NLT

When I have a family of my own,
I want to continue these
traditions:

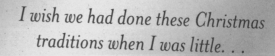

*I wish we had done these Christmas
traditions when I was little. . .*

....

....

....

....

....

....

....

....

....

....

....

....

....

....

....

....

How will you keep the Christmas story
fresh in the years to come?

Christmas Vacations You Dream about Taking

Parent Quiz: Kids, what are your parents' favorite parts of Christmas? (Parents, check to see if they're right!)

Write a prayer reflecting on this passage:

You shall love the LORD your God with all your heart and with all your soul and with all your might. And these words that I command you today shall be on your heart. You shall teach them diligently to your children, and shall talk of them when you sit in your house, and when you walk by the way, and when you lie down, and when you rise.

DEUTERONOMY 6:5–7 ESV

Peace on Earth

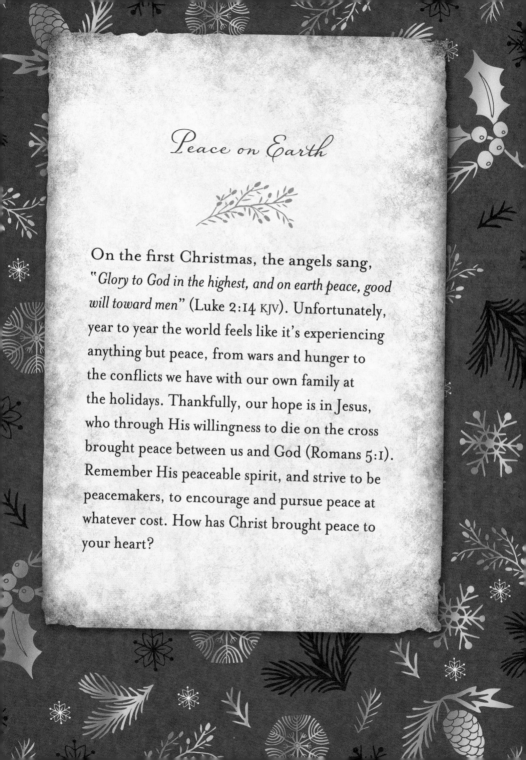

On the first Christmas, the angels sang, *"Glory to God in the highest, and on earth peace, good will toward men"* (Luke 2:14 KJV). Unfortunately, year to year the world feels like it's experiencing anything but peace, from wars and hunger to the conflicts we have with our own family at the holidays. Thankfully, our hope is in Jesus, who through His willingness to die on the cross brought peace between us and God (Romans 5:1). Remember His peaceable spirit, and strive to be peacemakers, to encourage and pursue peace at whatever cost. How has Christ brought peace to your heart?

" 'What means this glory round our feet,'
The Magi mused, 'more bright than morn!'
And voices chanted clear and sweet,
'To-day the Prince of Peace is born.' "

Lowell
"Christmas Carol"

Memories of When Your Family Was Given Christ's Peace during Hardship

....
....
....
....
....
....
....
....
....
....
....
....
....
....
....
....
....
....
....

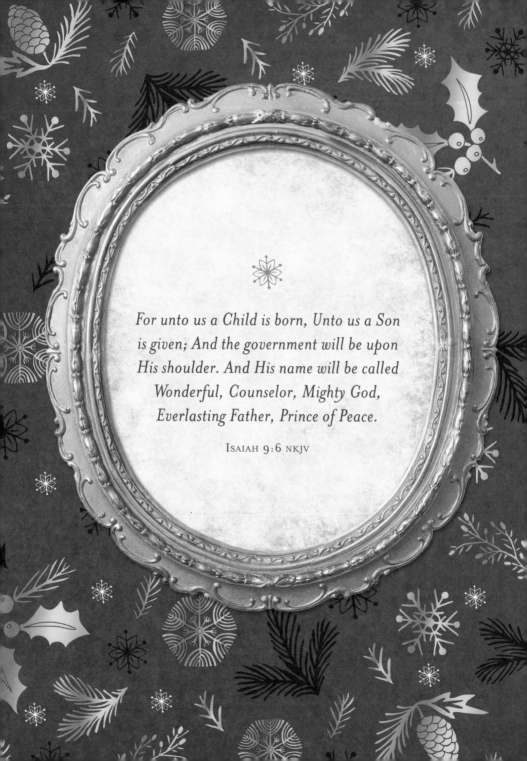

For unto us a Child is born, Unto us a Son is given; And the government will be upon His shoulder. And His name will be called Wonderful, Counselor, Mighty God, Everlasting Father, Prince of Peace.

ISAIAH 9:6 NKJV

Where have you felt Christ's peace at Christmas?

And let the peace of Christ rule in your hearts, to which indeed you were called in one body. And be thankful.

COLOSSIANS 3:15 ESV

How can you encourage
"peace on earth" at Christmas?

....
....
....
....
....
....
....
....
....
....
....
....
....
....
....
....
....
....
....

Write a prayer asking for Christ's peace
to envelop the hearts of your family,
the Church, and the world,
at Christmas and throughout the year.

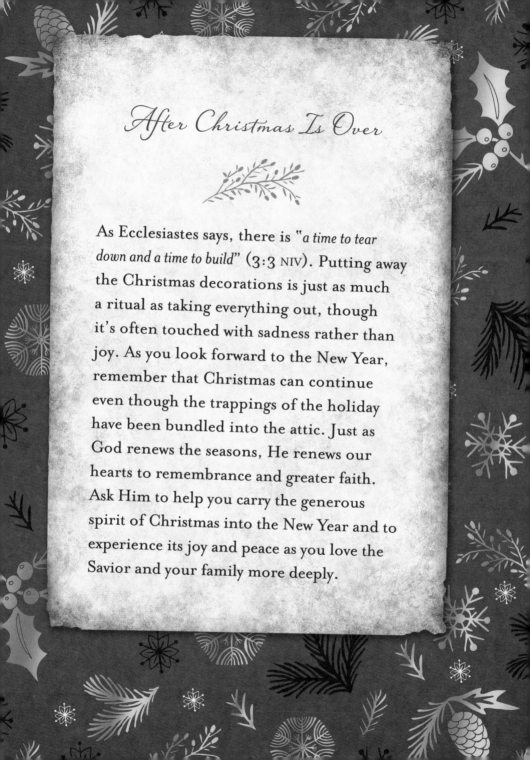

After Christmas Is Over

As Ecclesiastes says, there is *"a time to tear down and a time to build"* (3:3 NIV). Putting away the Christmas decorations is just as much a ritual as taking everything out, though it's often touched with sadness rather than joy. As you look forward to the New Year, remember that Christmas can continue even though the trappings of the holiday have been bundled into the attic. Just as God renews the seasons, He renews our hearts to remembrance and greater faith. Ask Him to help you carry the generous spirit of Christmas into the New Year and to experience its joy and peace as you love the Savior and your family more deeply.

"I will honor Christmas in my heart,
and try to keep it all the year."

EBENEZER SCROOGE
A CHRISTMAS CAROL BY CHARLES DICKENS

Taking Down the Tree and Other Decorations

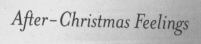

After-Christmas Feelings

Special Preparations for New Year's Celebrations

Fun with Family and Friends at New Year's

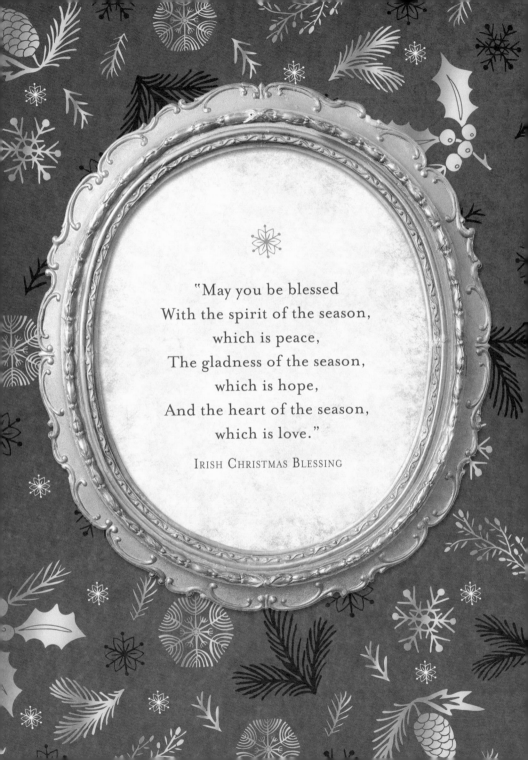

"May you be blessed
With the spirit of the season,
which is peace,
The gladness of the season,
which is hope,
And the heart of the season,
which is love."

IRISH CHRISTMAS BLESSING

Write a prayer asking God to help you
keep the spirit of Christmas alive
in your heart all year round.

Our Prayers for the New Year

....
....
....
....
....
....
....
....
....
....
....
....
....
....
....
....